The Healthy Heart Challenge

written by
Michelle Lombardo, D.C.

illustrated by
M.R. Herron

INCORPORATED

Copyright © 2000, 2007 by The OrganWise Guys Incorporated, 3838 Song River Circle, Duluth, GA 30097 Phone (800) 786-1730
www.organwiseguys.com
All rights reserved. No portion of this publication may be reproduced or transmitted in any form or by any means, without prior written permission from the publisher. ISBN: 0-9648438-7-0 Printed in the United States of America.
The OrganWise Guys® are registered trademarks of The OrganWise Guys Incorporated. Specific characters include: Hardy Heart®, Madame Muscle®, Windy®, Peri Stolic®, Calci M. Bone®, Sir Rebrum®, Peter Pancreas®, Pepto, Sid Kidney®, Kid Kidney®, The Kidney Brothers®, Luigi Liver®, and any other "Marks" that may be created by The OrganWise Guys Incorporated.

Hello! It's me, Hardy Heart, leader of The OrganWise Guys Club. Some of you may have heard about us. We are a group of organs. That's right, "organs" that live inside human beings. Our mission is to help kids understand how amazing the human body is and what they can do to keep their body in tip-top shape. Anyone who is dedicated to keeping us healthy is welcome to join. We're looking for new members, especially since we just remodeled the clubhouse! Let me tell you about one of our most recent adventures.

It was a beautiful Sunday afternoon and we had just returned from a 2-mile hike. On Sundays, we like to chill out and have fun. What makes us unique is that we all enjoy our own interests and hobbies. After a good workout, I love to swing on the hammock and think about how great I feel!

Windy, the lungs, was doing one of her favorite things, painting. She really has a gift for art. Landscapes and skies are her specialties. For some reason, she really likes the whole "fresh air" thing! She is a firm believer in keeping lungs "smoke free!"

Luigi Liver, Peter Pancreas and Peri Stolic, the intestines, were busy in the garden. Peri Stolic is so proud of the pumpkin they grew. They are entering a local contest in a couple of days to compete for the largest pumpkin in the county. I think they have a pretty good shot at winning!

Calci M. Bone and Madame Muscle were busy putting the finishing touches on a dance routine for the cheerleaders at the local school.

Inside the clubhouse, Sir Rebrum was, as usual, surfing the web. He is like a sponge when it comes to information. Sid and Kid were playing their new video game, *WaterSports*. As long as water is involved, the Kidney Brothers are interested!

Pepto was doing what he does best... trying out a new recipe. We all like his hobby because when he finds a healthy recipe, we all get to sample it fresh out of the oven!

I was ready to doze off when I heard Sir Rebrum calling my name. He seemed quite concerned about something. I ran in to make sure everything was okay.

"Hardy, you are not going to believe what I just found on the web!" gasped Sir Rebrum. "I was looking up the latest research on CARDIOVASCULAR DISEASE and I found that it can affect me, the brain! How is that possible? I think there has been a mistake. I know "cardio" means "heart," "vascular" means "arteries and veins," and disease means well, you know, sickness! I understand all that, but then I came to the word STROKE. The research goes on to talk about me, the brain!"

By this time, Sir Rebrum was in a panic. What he was saying was right. Cardiovascular disease does affect more than just the heart. Being a heart, I admit that I focus on keeping hearts healthy because, honestly, it can be kind of depressing if I think what my fate *could* be. That's when I reminded Sir Rebrum of the reason we formed The OrganWise Guys Club; to help kids stay healthy. I suggested we teach kids all about cardiovascular disease and stroke and what they can do to prevent it!

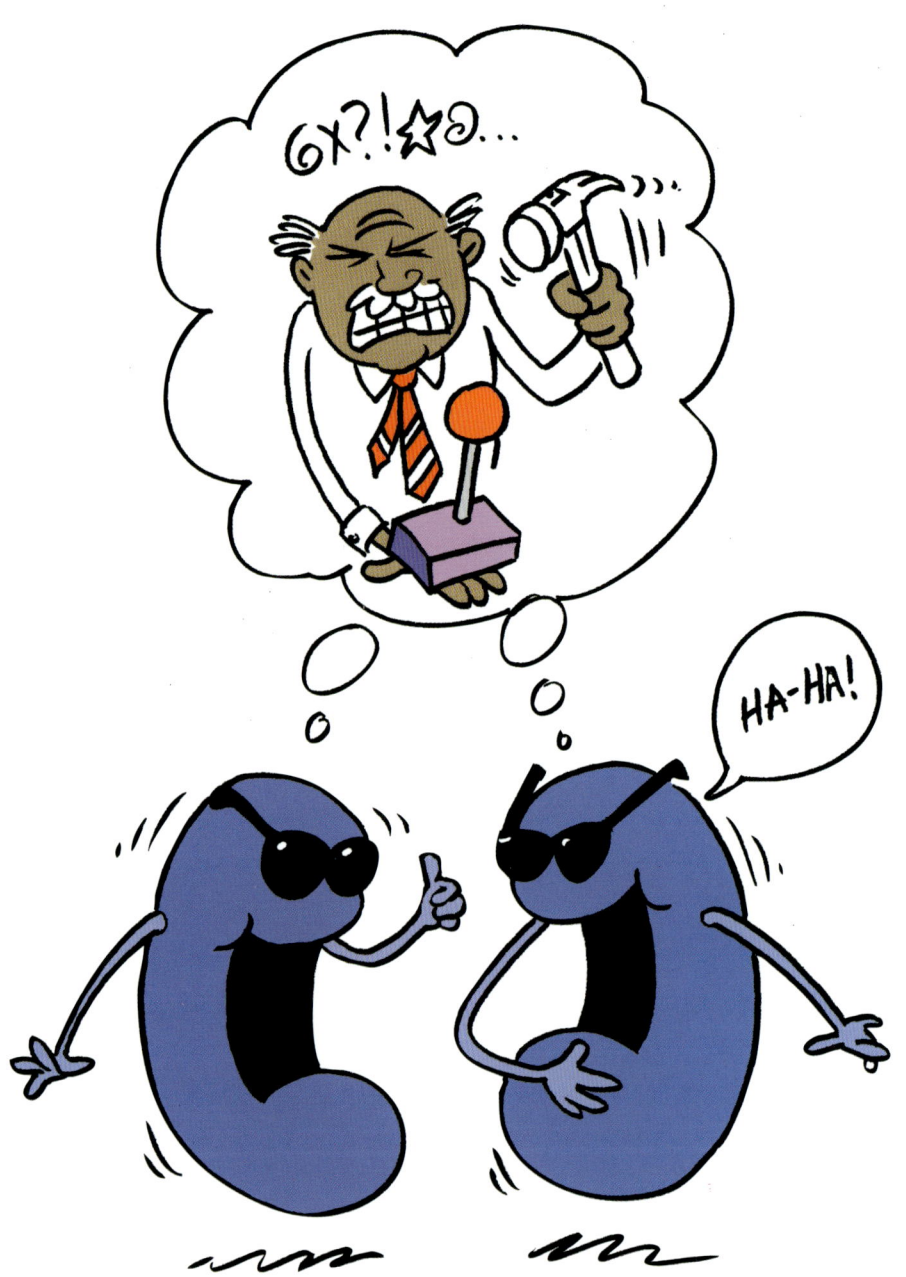

That's when Kid chimed in. "Are you kidding? That stuff is way too complicated for kids! Big words like that are for doctors. I can hardly pronounce them!"

Now this got Sir Rebrum thinking (which is nothing unusual!). "Kids are a lot smarter than you think," he said. "Those video games you're playing are great examples. Kids can figure them out in no time. Have you ever seen an adult try to play? It really is kind of funny! I agree with Hardy. What we need to do is break it down and explain it in a way kids can understand. Remember my favorite saying - *Knowledge is power.*"

"I'll wait until you come out with the 'cardio-whatever' video game," Kid said with a smirk on his face. "Kids are too young to know about that kind of doctor stuff," he continued.

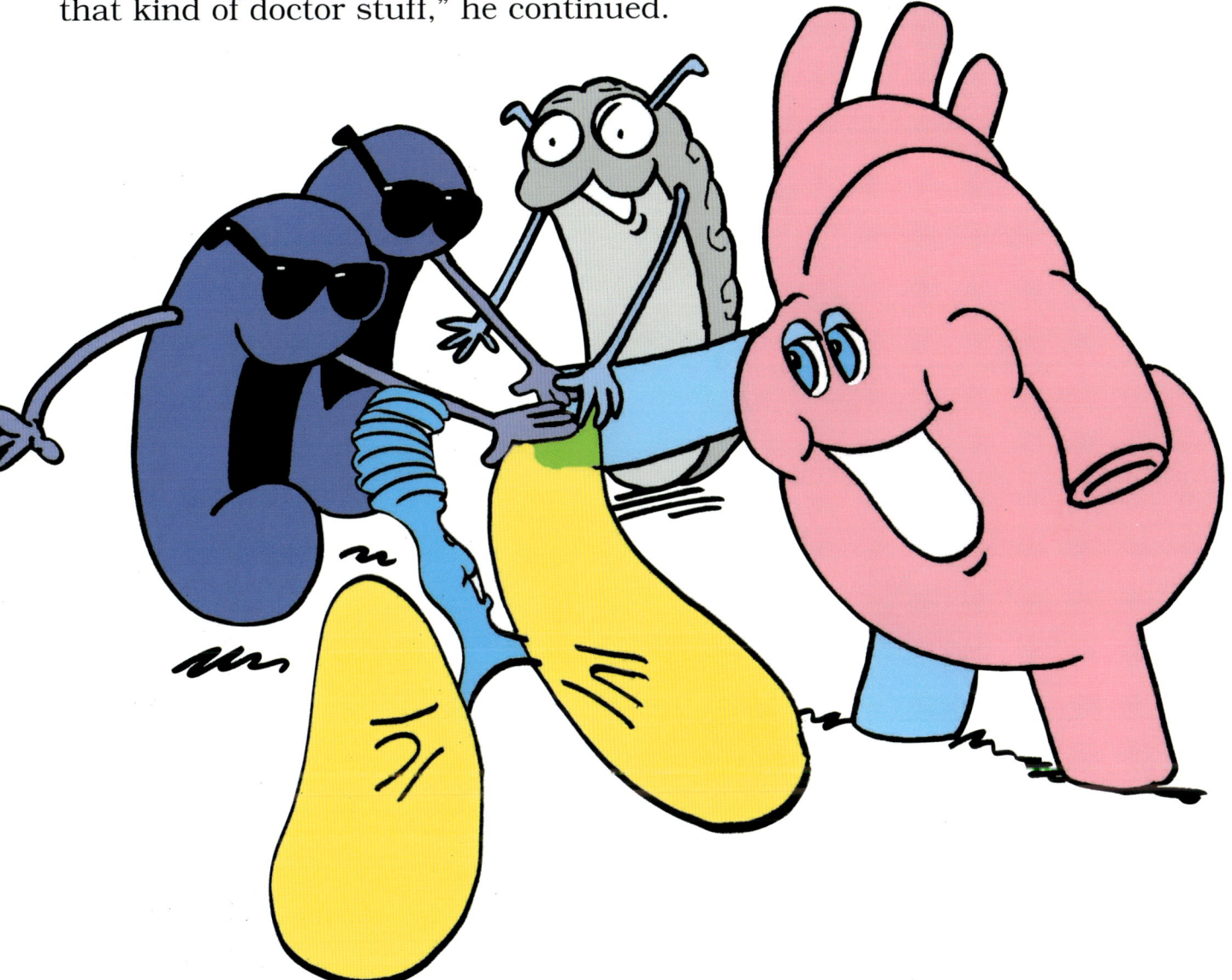

"Sounds like a challenge to me!" said Sir Rebrum. "I know how much grey matter kids have. Just then Windy flew up. "I'm in!" she said, "I've been trying to let kids know how bad smoking is, not only for me, the lungs, but also how damaging it is for Hardy and Sir Rebrum! I bet that Hardy, Sir Rebrum and I can get a classroom of kids to not only pronounce cardiovascular disease, but also understand what it means and how to prevent it!" "You're on!" said Kid. The five of us shook on it as we all agreed that the winners would be treated to a banana split. We had our work cut out for us, but Sir Rebrum, Windy and I knew we would succeed!

We were sure that Mrs. Jones, a teacher at the school down the street, would let us come in and teach this valuable information to her class.

The three of us spent the rest of the afternoon putting a presentation together for Mrs. Jones' class. We knew there was a lot more than a banana split riding on this project. The health of children was at stake! And when it comes to the health of children, The OrganWise Guys mean serious business.

The presentation day arrived. Mrs. Jones set aside an hour for our program. We were a little nervous getting up in front of the class. I went first. "Have you ever heard of cardiovascular disease?" I asked. They all looked at me as if I were speaking a foreign language. Maybe Sid and Kid were right! As I began to sweat, someone in the back of the room raised his hand.

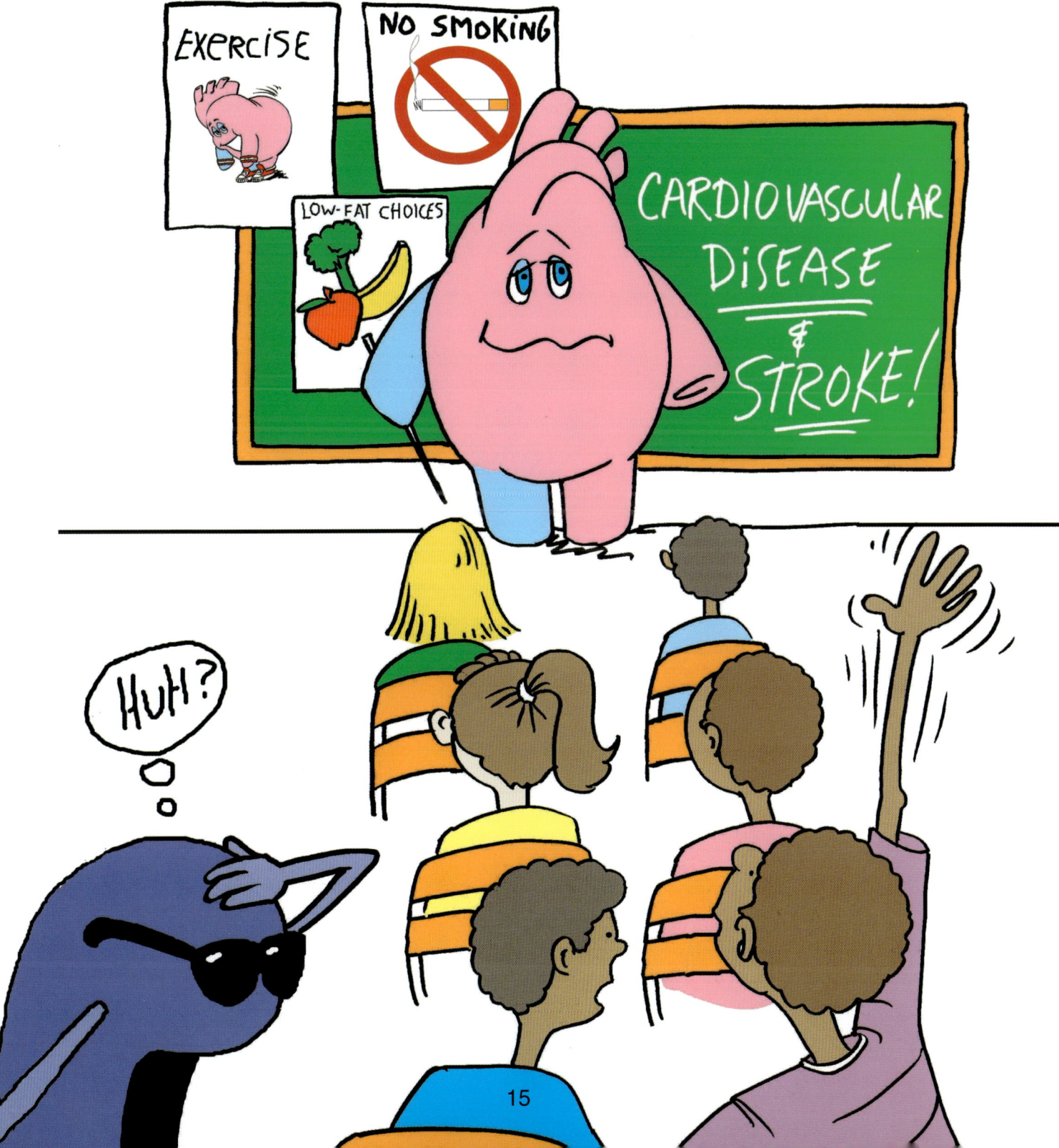

"I've heard of it," said Johnny. "My grandpa went to the doctor yesterday and brought home information about it. I heard him talking to my grandma about making some healthy changes. The first thing he planned to do was to throw out his cigarettes and finally quit the bad habit of smoking! He sounded pretty serious. He talked about how special his family is and then came over and gave me a big hug. I figured it had something to do with the *heart*, because he kept saying how much he loved me!"

Well, that was all I needed. I wasn't sweating anymore, now I was almost crying! "That's exactly right, Johnny; it is about the heart! Let me break it down for you." I wrote the following on the chalkboard:

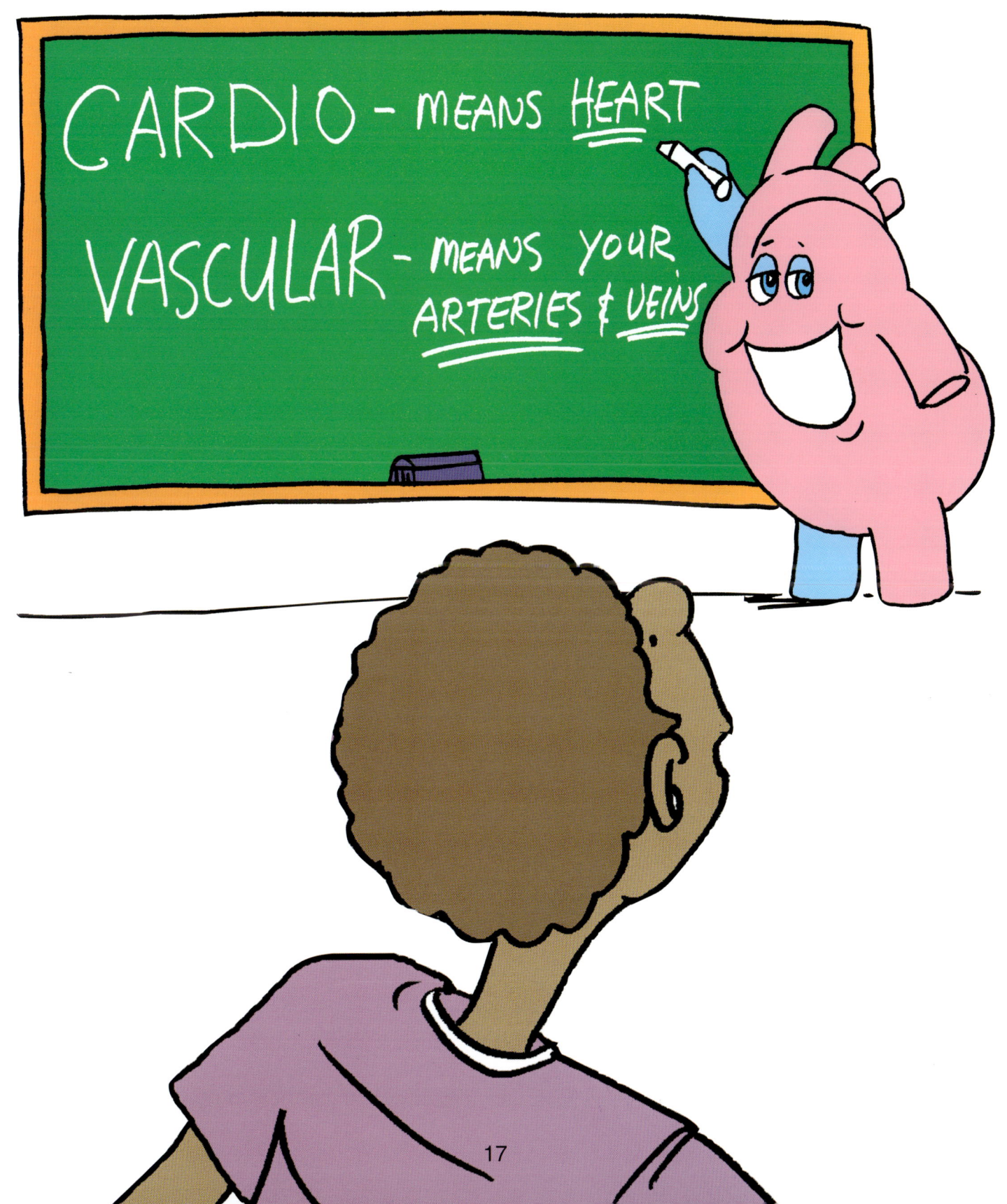

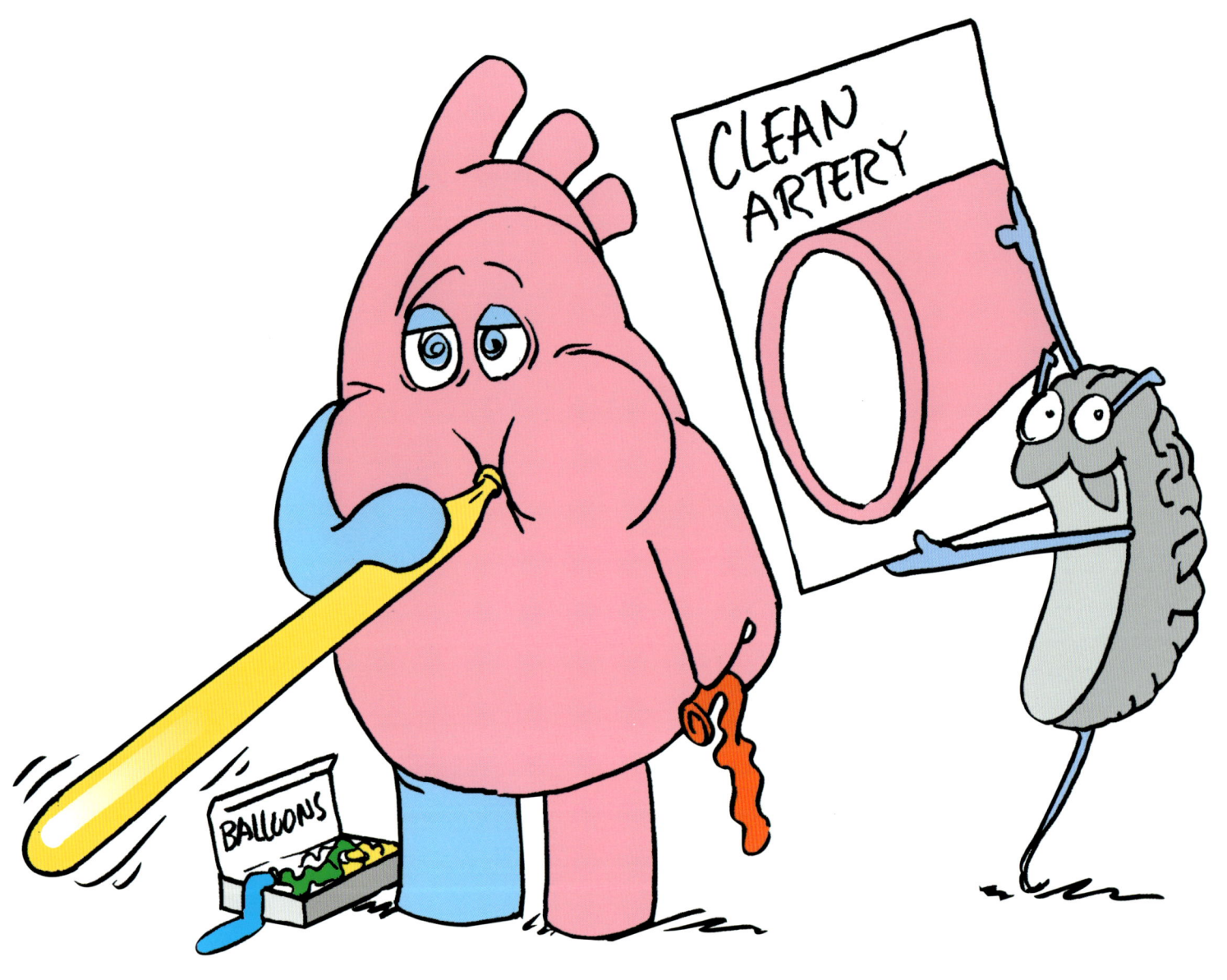

"Let me explain," I said with excitement in my voice. "Your arteries and veins are like those long balloons that clowns tie into animal shapes. They are the tubes that carry blood to every part of your body. Some are large and some are very tiny. When you are born, they are clean as a whistle on the inside."

"As you humans go through life, you can help keep your arteries clean by making healthy choices everyday; or you can let them, shall we say, "go down the tubes." They can become clogged just like an old rusty pipe! It's up to you! Let's take a look at what can happen to me and to Sir Rebrum when these tubes get clogged."

HEART ATTACK

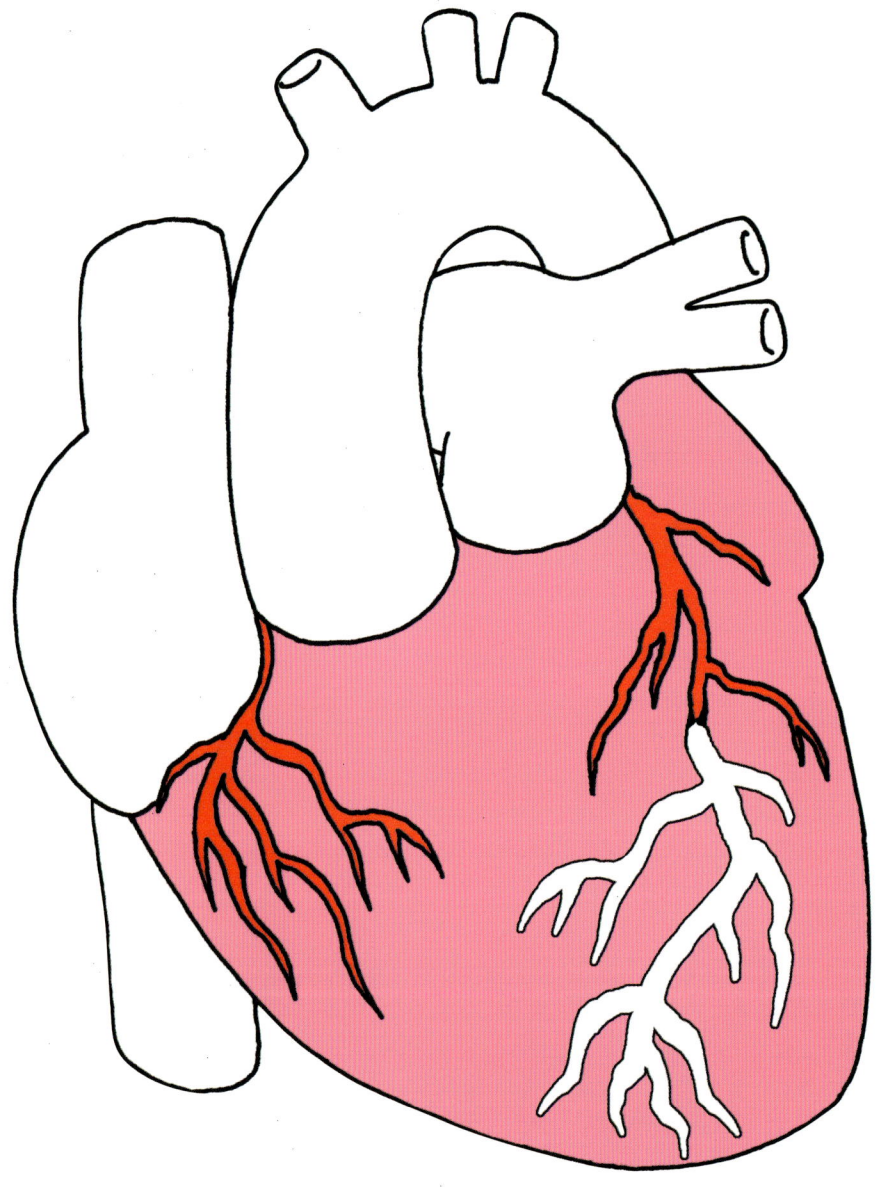

"For me, the heart, it's called a HEART ATTACK. It's a strange name because it isn't as if someone is attacking me! The arteries (tubes) that feed blood to the heart muscle are tiny ones. If one of these tubes gets clogged so much that blood can't get through, I have trouble pumping! This is a HEART ATTACK! I don't mean to brag, but it's this pumping action that keeps you humans alive! Yet, cardiovascular disease can affect more than just me, the heart."

"Now on to my friend, Sir Rebrum. Blood is like fuel for your brain. When the tiny arteries that feed the brain get clogged, the blood can't get through. This is called a STROKE. I don't think I need to explain how important it is to keep blood going to your brain!"

"Don't let the big words scare you. The important fact to remember is that we must keep our arteries and veins healthy so that blood flows to the two most important organs in your body, Sir Rebrum and me, Hardy Heart."

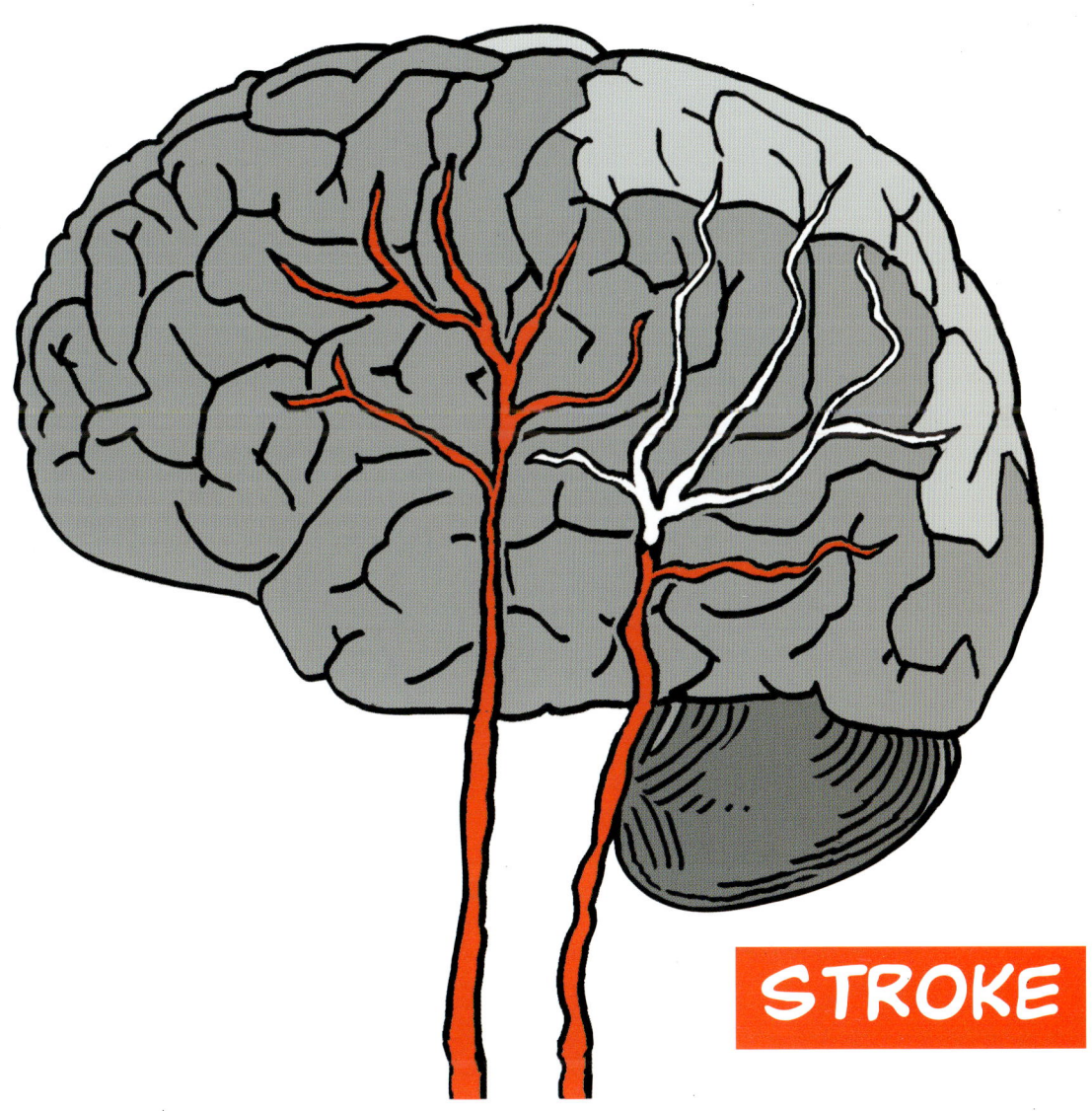

That's when the students began firing questions at me. I was so relieved! I knew they would be interested once they understood! "How do the tubes get clogged?" asked one. "Is there anything we can do about it?" questioned another. "What about our parents and grandparents who may already have some clogging?" "Does this happen to everyone?" "Does smoking make things worse?" "Does being physically active help keep the arteries from clogging?" You should have seen the look on Sid and Kid's faces!

We only had a few minutes left. If Sir Rebrum, Windy and I were going to win this challenge I had to answer these questions quickly. I started talking about how the tubes get clogged. "Making too many high-fat food choices combined with too much sitting around is how it starts."

"If a person eats lots of butter, fried foods, potato chips and other high-fat snacks every single day, the body produces bad cholesterol. Of course, we all have these foods once in while, but don't make a steady diet of them! This bad cholesterol is what builds up on the inside of the arteries and veins causing them to clog."

"So what should you do? Choose foods with less fat. Start with simple steps such as skipping the butter on those healthy vegetables, having grilled chicken instead of fried chicken, and choosing snacks like pretzels, apples, oranges, bananas and yogurt. These simple changes can make a huge difference in the health of your arteries and veins!"

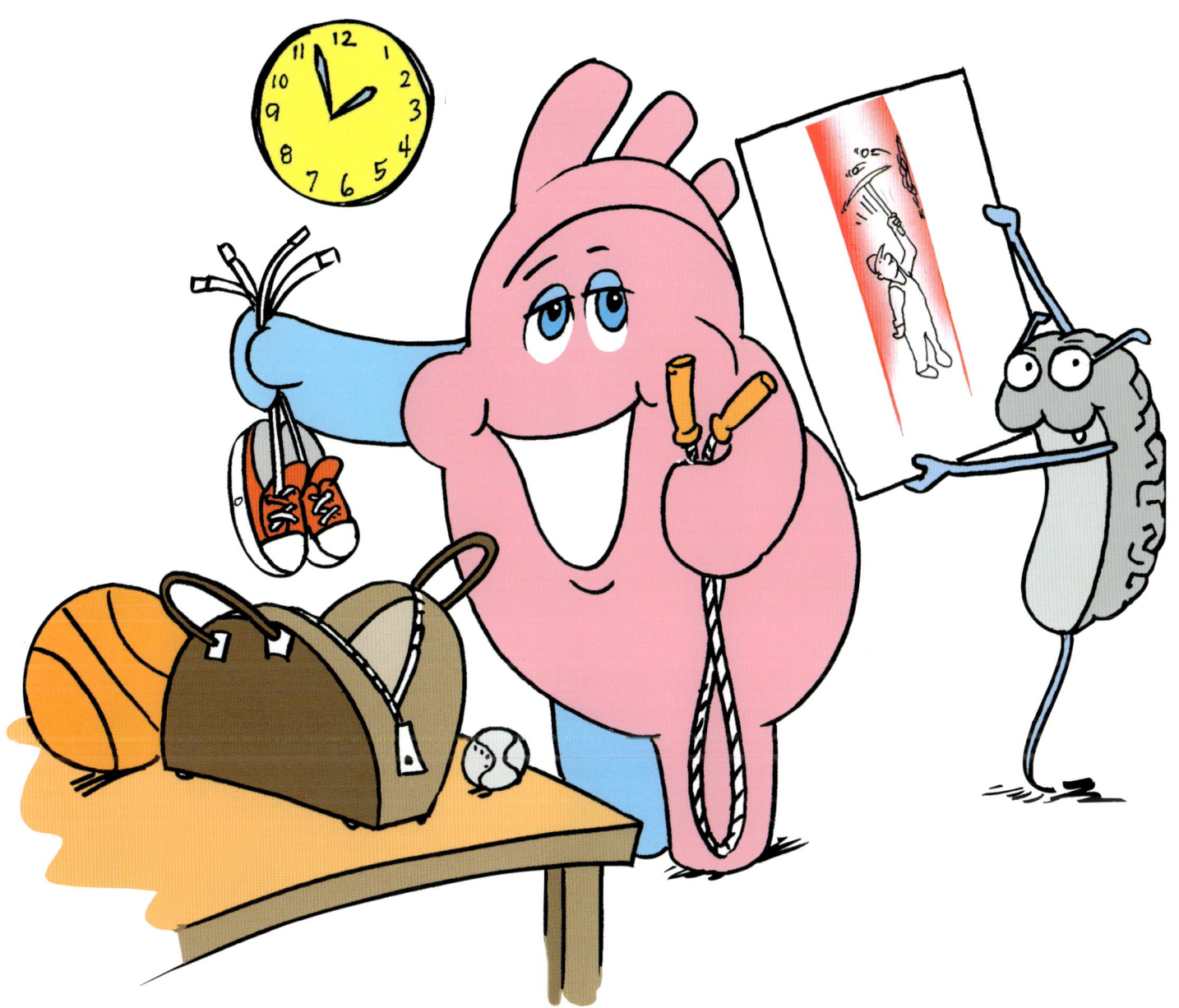

"What else can you do? Get moving! The OrganWise Guys love it when you play outside, ride bikes, take walks, dance, swim, play sports or do any other activity. When you are physically active your body makes good cholesterol. Good cholesterol is like having little workers inside your arteries and veins chipping away at the bad cholesterol and cleaning up your arteries."

And thirdly, never smoke. Take a look as Windy points out what cigarette smoke does once it gets inside the lungs. This smoke causes large numbers of "free radicals." These "free radicals" are out to do damage to many parts of your body including your arteries and veins. Smoking raises a person's blood pressure which can lead to a heart attack or stroke! Smoking is one of the most damaging bad habits a person could have. And it's not just the person who smokes that can have serious problems. Second-hand smoke, which is the smoke that one breathes in from being in a place where a person is smoking, also causes damage! Did you know that the same chemicals found in nail polish remover, poison, swamp gas, rocket fuel and lighter fluid are also found in tobacco products and secondhand smoke? These chemicals are especially harmful to children! There is nothing that gets Windy more "fired up" than when she sees an adult smoking in a closed-in area where there are children.

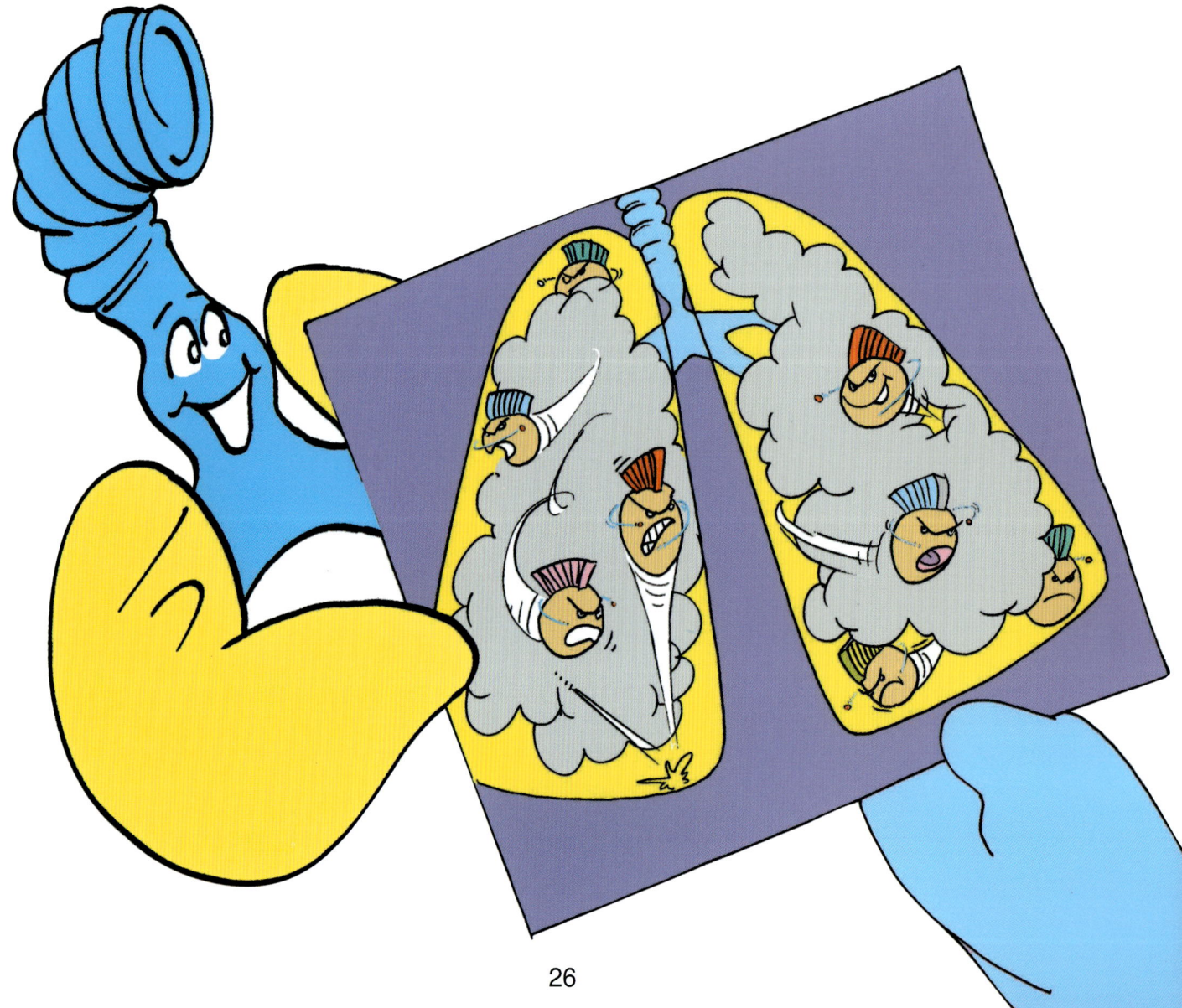

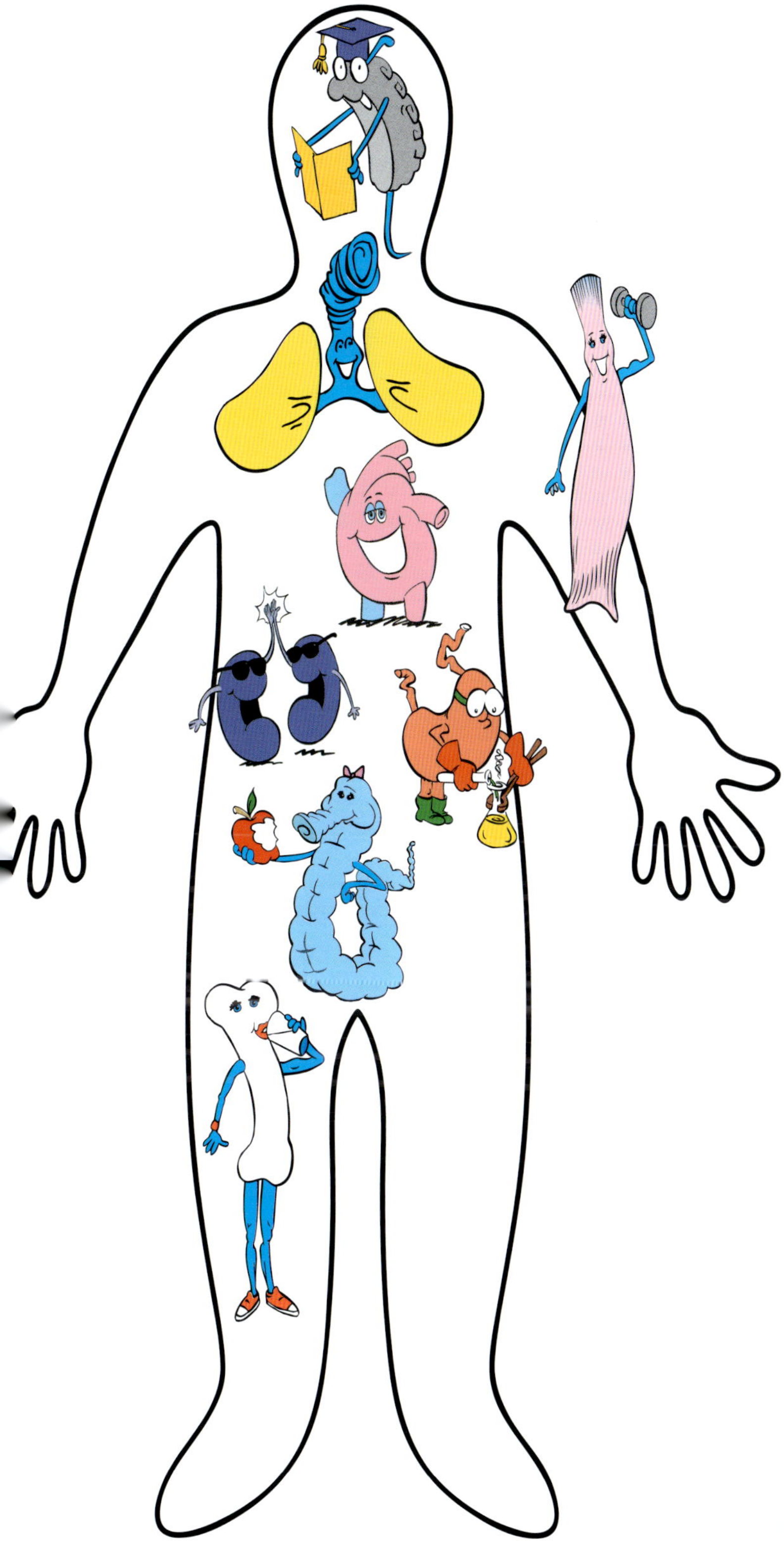

"Let me answer your question about "who can be affected by cardiovascular disease?" The answer is anyone with unhealthy daily habits. But certain groups of people seem to have more cases of cardiovascular disease as compared to others. Studies are underway to try to understand this. Just remember though, that no matter what color a person is on the outside, we OrganWise Guys are still the same on the inside. Our motto for everyone is: "We love who we live in, so please take care of us!" Making healthy choices are important no matter which race you belong to or what age you are. Remember Johnny's grandpa who decided to quit smoking? Even someone his age can improve because it is never too late to take charge of your health!"

With only two minutes left, it was time to test the kids. "Let's see what you have learned today about cardiovascular disease and stroke," Sir Rebrum said confidently. He could almost taste the banana split! Hardy handed out the Healthy Heart Challenge questions. The class had only a few minutes to answer the questions. (See if you can answer these questions too, but don't write in this book. Either say it out loud or write your answers on another sheet of paper.)

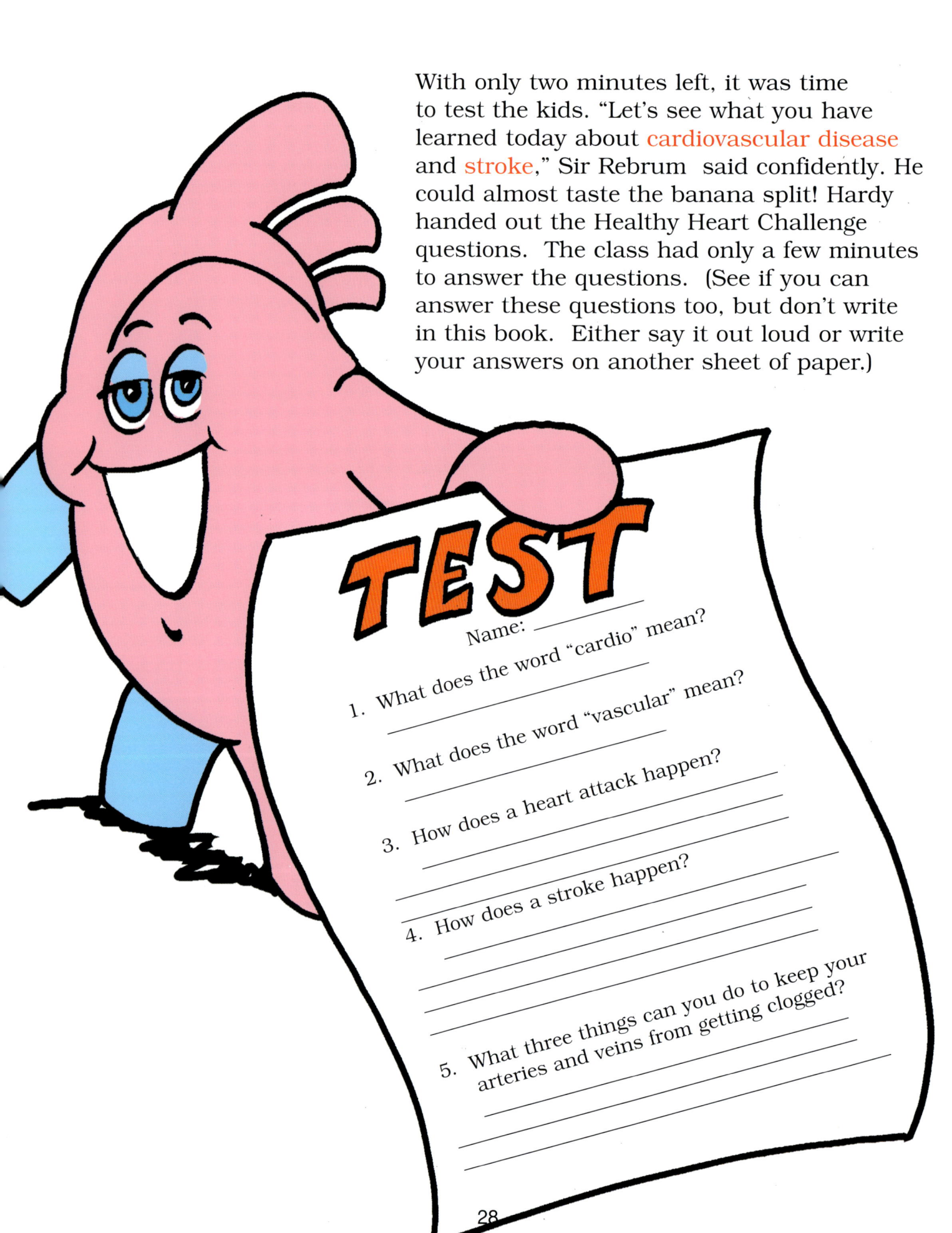

TEST

Name: _____

1. What does the word "cardio" mean?

2. What does the word "vascular" mean?

3. How does a heart attack happen?

4. How does a stroke happen?

5. What three things can you do to keep your arteries and veins from getting clogged?

Hardy and Sir Rebrum collected all of the papers. Johnny's paper was the last one to be graded. If all his questions are answered correctly, everyone in the class will have passed. Check Johnny's answers to see how he did.

TEST

Name: **JOHNNY**

1. What does the word "cardio" mean?
   HEART

2. What does the word "vascular" mean?
   YOUR ARTERIES AND VEINS (TUBES)

3. How does a heart attack happen?
   AN ARTERY THAT CARRIES BLOOD TO THE HEART GETS CLOGGED SO THE HEART HAS TROUBLE PUMPING!

4. How does a stroke happen?
   AN ARTERY THAT CARRIES BLOOD TO THE BRAIN GETS CLOGGED SO THAT PART OF THE BRAIN CAN'T THINK ANYMORE!

5. What three things can you do to keep your arteries and veins from getting clogged?
   CHOOSE FOODS WITH LESS FAT
   GET PLENTY OF PHYSICAL ACTIVITY (EXERCISE)
   NEVER SMOKE CIGARETTES

He did it - 100%! Sid and Kid were sitting in the back of the room in amazement. Sir Rebrum was right, kids are smart!

The following day we rode our bikes to the Dairy Barn for banana splits (with low-fat frozen yogurt, of course!). Windy flew along as we rode. I couldn't wait to taste the delicious bananas and fresh strawberries, especially since The Kidney Brothers were buying! Kid was grinning from ear to ear. I asked him why he was so happy since he didn't win the challenge.

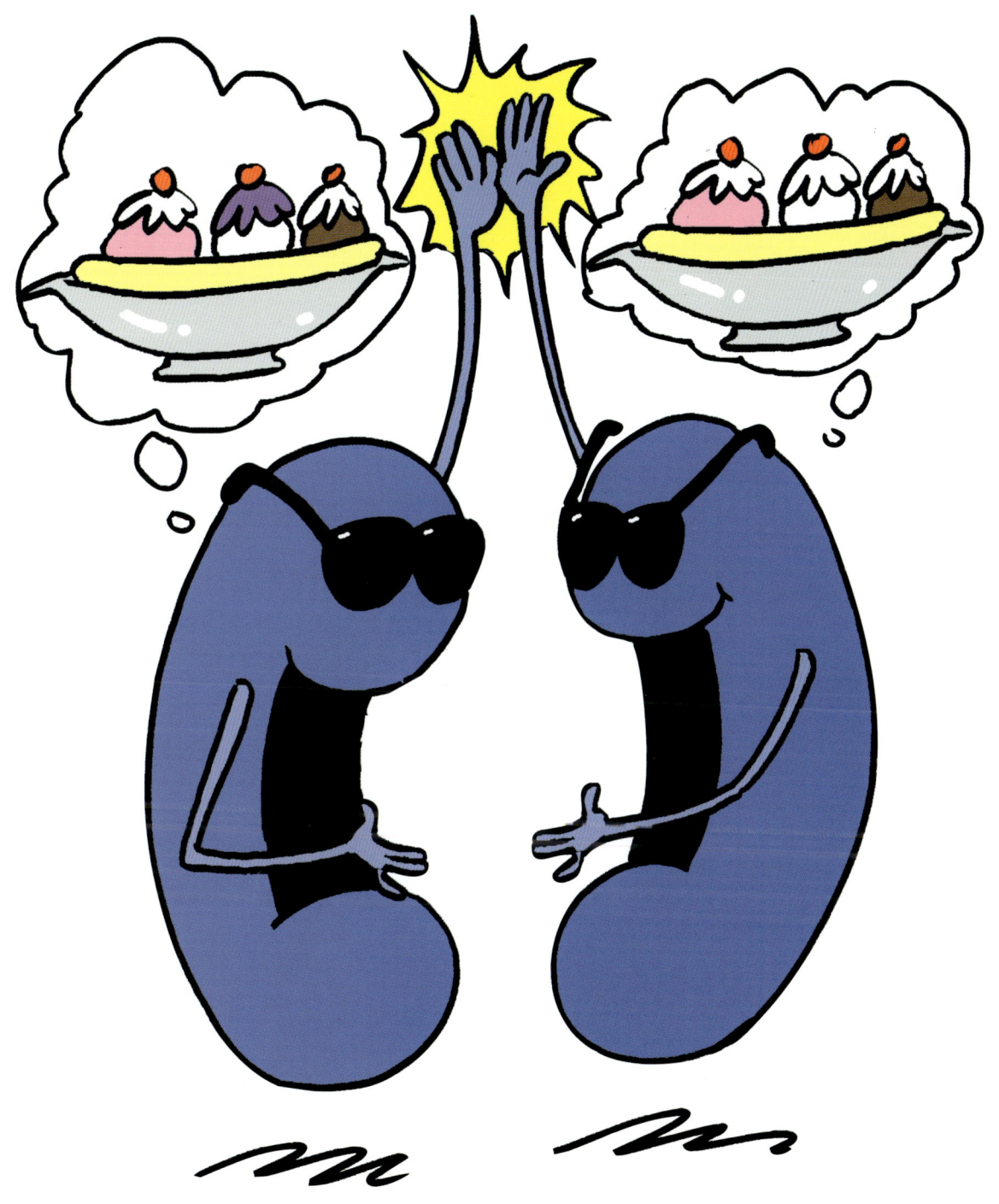

"It was a win-win situation for us," said Kid as he gave Sid their famous "high five." "We learned as much as the class did about cardiovascular disease. We also get our blood supply from arteries, so we're all for keeping them clean! And whether we won or lost the challenge, we knew we were going to get banana splits either way!"

I started laughing as I remembered Kid telling us that kids weren't that smart. But I have to be honest; Sir Rebrum, Windy and I were pretty impressed with how much the kids learned. It used to be that only doctors knew all this stuff. But the truth is, we all have a "doctor" inside of us. The human body is amazing and can work to help keep itself healthy if it is given the right tools. Make healthy eating and regular physical activity part of your daily routine. And remember, don't ever smoke cigarettes or use any other tobacco products. The Organwise Guys are counting on you so we can live a long and healthy life because "we love you, man!"

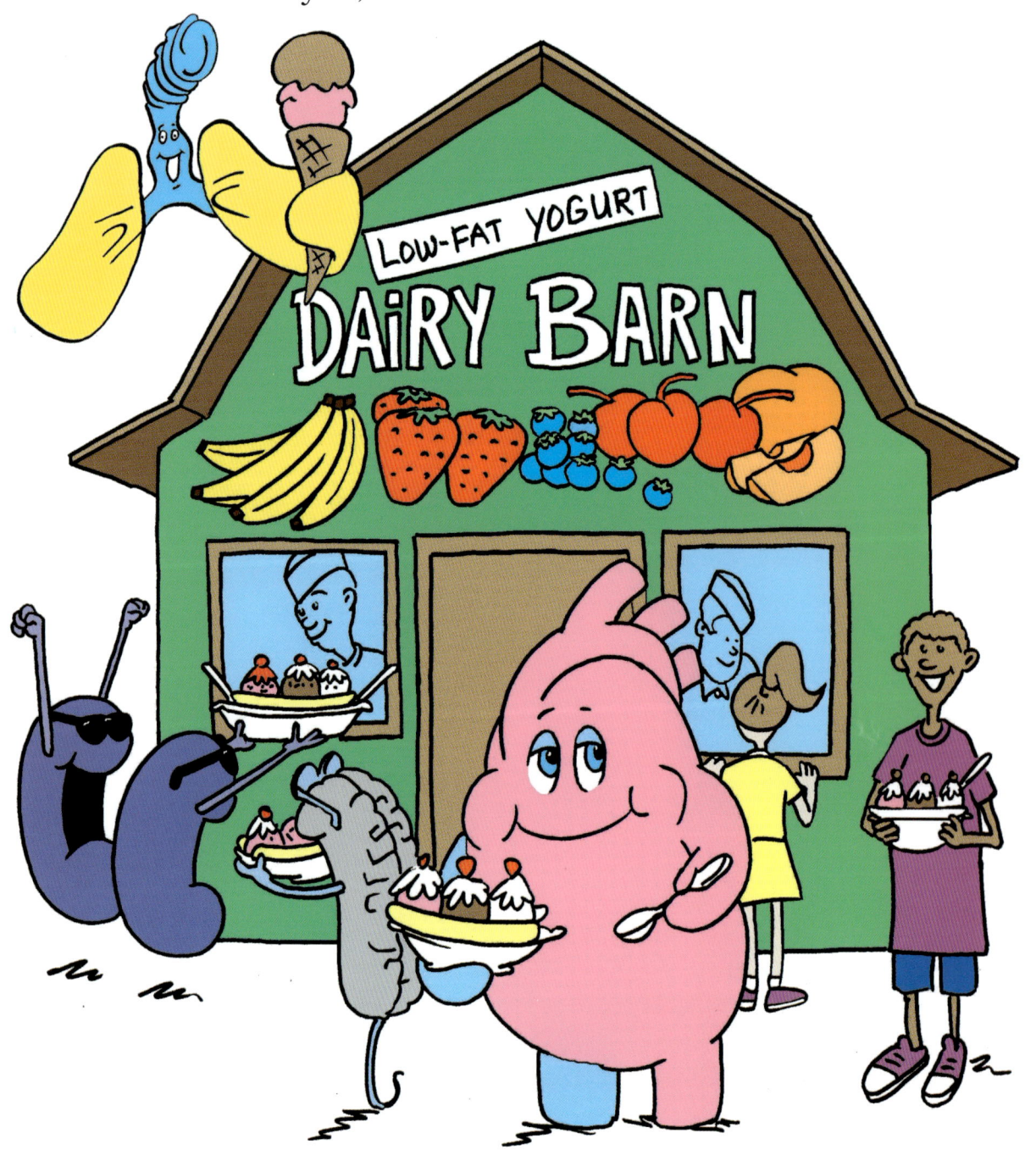